EXPERIMENTS WITH SIMPLE MACHINES

A TRUE BOOK®

by

Salvatore Tocci

Children's Press®

A Division of Scholastic Inc.

New York Toronto London Auckland Sydney
Mexico City New Delhi Hong Kong
Danbury, Connecticut

These children are playing on a seesaw. A seesaw is a simple machine.

Reading Consultant
Susan Virgilio

Science Consultant
Robert Gardner

The photo on the cover shows gears. The photo on the title page shows a pulley.

The author and publisher are not responsible for injuries or accidents that occur during or from any experiments. Experiments should be conducted in the presence of or with the help of an adult. Any instructions of the experiments that require the use of sharp, hot, or other unsafe items should be conducted by or with the help of an adult.

Library of Congress Cataloging-in-Publication Data

Tocci, Salvatore.
   Experiments with simple machines / Salvatore Tocci.
   p. cm. – (A true book)
   Summary: Describes various kinds of simple machines, showing how they can be made out of easily obtainable objects and detailing experiments that show how they make tasks easier to perform.
Includes bibliographical references and index.
  ISBN 0-516-22604-5 (lib. bdg.) 0-516-27468-6 (pbk.)
   1. Simple Machines—Juvenile literature. [1. Simple Machines—Experiments. 2. Experiments.] I. Title.
TJ147 .T57 2003
621.8'078—dc21

2002001595

CHILDREN'S PRESS, AND A TRUE BOOK®, and associated logos are trademarks and or registered trademarks of Grolier Publishing Co., Inc. SCHOLASTIC and associated logos are trademarks and or registered trademarks of Scholastic Inc.
    4 5 6 7 8 9 10 R 12 11 10 09 08 07 06

Contents

No More Oversleeping

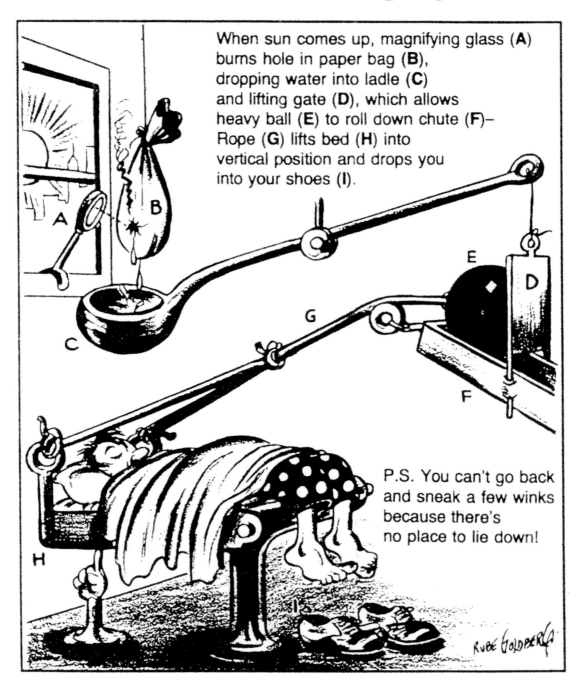

When sun comes up, magnifying glass (**A**) burns hole in paper bag (**B**), dropping water into ladle (**C**) and lifting gate (**D**), which allows heavy ball (**E**) to roll down chute (**F**)— Rope (**G**) lifts bed (**H**) into vertical position and drops you into your shoes (**I**).

P.S. You can't go back and sneak a few winks because there's no place to lie down!

RUBE GOLDBERG

What Time Is It?

Do you usually have trouble getting up in the morning to get ready for school? Then you may need something special to wake you up, like the gadget shown on the opposite page. This gadget is called a Rube Goldberg device. Goldberg was a popular cartoonist who lived from 1883 to 1970. For almost fifty years, he drew cartoons like the one on page 4. Each cartoon showed a very complicated device that did a very simple task. Obviously, his devices were meant to be funny.

Today, Rube Goldberg contests are held every year throughout the country for students of all ages. The challenge is to build a device that uses a lot of steps to

carry out a simple task. One
winning entry took more than
forty steps just to pick, clean,
and peel an apple.

Although they look complicated, all Rube Goldberg devices are assembled from items that you can find at home. These devices, like the one shown on the previous page, also use **simple machines**. To learn about simple machines, you don't have to build a Rube Goldberg device. All you have to do is carry out the experiments in this book.

What Is a Simple Machine?

A Rube Goldberg device deliberately uses simple machines to make a simple task much more complicated. In other words, the machines make work harder. This is exactly what machines are not supposed to do. A machine

9

is designed to make work easier. Machines can be huge and very complex. They can also be small and simple. These are known as simple machines. See how a simple machine makes work much easier.

Lifting It Up

You will need:
- six thin books that are about the same size
- two unsharpened pencils

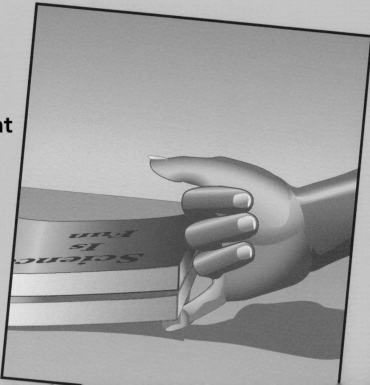

Place your little finger under the edge of one book. Try to lift the book. If you can lift one book, place another book on top of it. Can you lift the two books with your finger? If you can, keep adding one book at a time to see how many books you can lift with your finger.

Now place one pencil along the edge of one book. Place one end of the second pencil under the book and on top of the first pencil. Use your little finger to push down on the second pencil. Can you lift the book? Keep adding one book at a time to see how many books you can lift by pushing down on the pencil with your finger. What is the best spot to push on the pencil so that it is easiest to lift the books?

It is easier to lift the books by pressing on the pencil rather than it is to lift them with your finger. The two pencils act as a simple machine called a **lever**. The pencil you push with your finger is called the **lever arm**. The lever arm can move. The other pencil is known as the **fulcrum**. The fulcrum does not move. It is the point at which the lever arm moves. You will find it easier to lift the books by pushing down on the lever arm as far away from the fulcrum as possible.

Levers make all kinds of tasks easier to do. What other kinds of simple machines make work easier?

A crowbar is a lever that makes it easier to lift heavy objects.

Pulling It Together

You will need:
- two adults
- two brooms
- measuring tape
- rope

Ask the adults to stand about 2 feet (0.6 meters) apart, facing each other. Have each adult hold a broom handle horizontally at waist height. Stand between them. Tell the adults to hold onto the broom handles tightly while you try to pull them together. No matter how hard you pull, the adults should be able to keep the broom handles apart.

Now tie one end of the rope to one of the broom handles. Wrap the rope around the two broom handles three times. Have the adults hold the broom handles as they did before. Stand behind one of the adults. Challenge them to keep the broom handles apart while you pull on the rope.

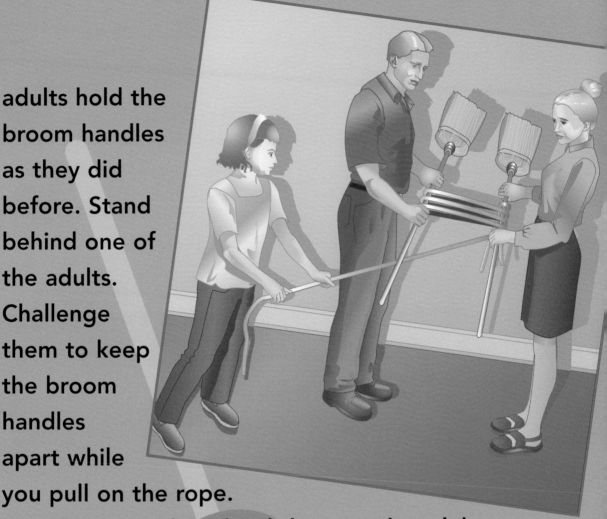

No matter how hard they try, the adults will not be able to keep the broom handles apart. The rope and broom handles act as another simple machine called a **pulley**.

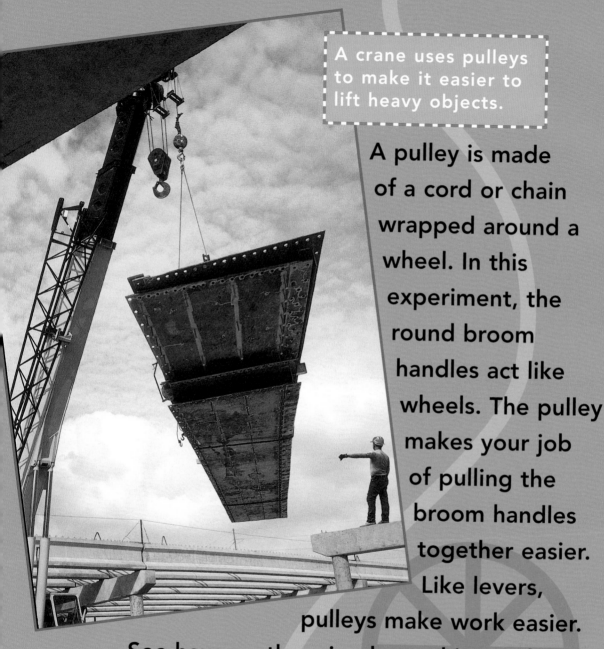

A crane uses pulleys to make it easier to lift heavy objects.

A pulley is made of a cord or chain wrapped around a wheel. In this experiment, the round broom handles act like wheels. The pulley makes your job of pulling the broom handles together easier. Like levers, pulleys make work easier. See how another simple machine makes it easier to move something.

Experiment 3

Sliding It Along

You will need:
- cup hook
- heavy wooden block
- table
- rubber band
- ruler
- long wooden board

Screw the cup hook into the top of the wooden block. Place the rubber band on the hook. Set the block on the floor and use the rubber band to lift it onto the table. Measure the length of the rubber band just before you put the block on the table.

Remove the hook from the block. Screw it into one of the shorter edges of the block.

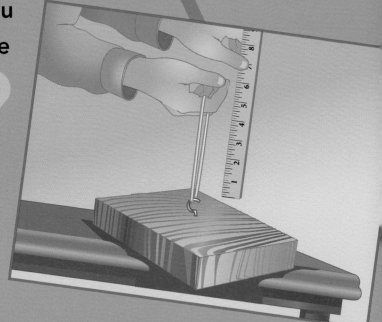

Rest the board against the table so that it slants like a ramp. Set the block at the bottom of the board. Use the rubber band to pull the block slowly up the board to the top of the table. Measure the length of the rubber band just before the block reaches the table.

You move the block the same height each time. But your job is easier when you slide it up the board. You can tell this because the rubber band does not stretch as much. The board acts as another simple machine called an **inclined plane.** Like all simple machines, inclined planes make work easier.

A ramp is an inclined plane that makes it easier to load a truck.

Where Are the Simple Machines in Your Home?

People at work are not the only ones who use simple machines to make their jobs easier. Even when they're at home, people use simple machines for all kinds of jobs. In fact, you can find a variety of simple machines right in your own home.

Experiment 4

Winding Around

You will need:
- ruler
- pencil
- paper
- scissors
- marker

Draw a right triangle on the paper. Make it 5 inches (13 centimeters) high and 9 inches (23 cm) along its bottom. Cut out the triangle. Use the marker to color the sloping edge of the triangle. Place the 5-inch (13-cm) edge of the paper against the pencil. Roll the pencil slowly so that the paper wraps around it evenly.

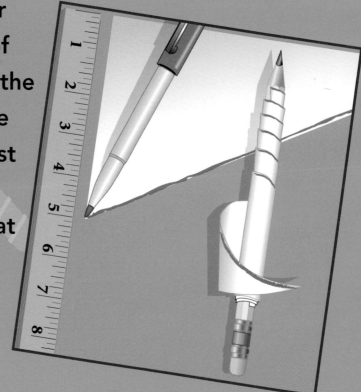

Look closely at how the colored edge of the paper goes up the pencil. This edge should look like an inclined plane that twists around the pencil from bottom to top. Now hold the pencil at arm's length. Does it remind you of anything? The pencil should look like a screw.

You know that screws are used to join things, such as pieces of wood. But did you know that a screw is also used to make work easier? A screw is a simple machine that is found in most homes.

By turning a screw that is part of a car jack, a person can lift a car off the ground easily.

A corkscrew is another example of an item that you may have at home that is a simple machine. By turning the corkscrew, a cork can be removed from a bottle easily. A variety of other kitchen devices are also simple machines. For example, both a "church key" opener and a nutcracker are examples of levers. What other simple machines can be found in your home?

These kitchen devices use simple tools to make jobs easier.

Breaking It Apart

You will need:
- an adult helper
- hammer
- finishing nail
- two wooden boards
- large nail

Ask an adult to help you hammer the finishing nail to join the two boards. Try to pull the boards apart with your hands. Unless you have super strength, you won't be able to do it.

Stand the boards on edge on the floor. Place the large nail between them. Use the hammer to hit the large nail gently. What happens to the boards?

After you hit the large nail, you find it much easier to separate the two boards.

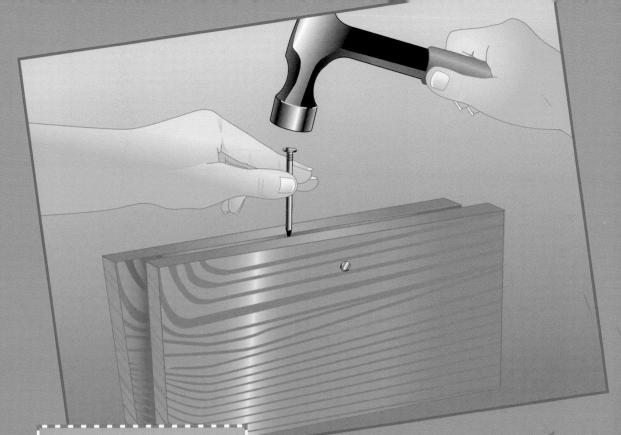

If you look closely at the sharp end of any nail, you'll see that it is shaped into a fine point. This point acts as a **wedge**. A wedge is a simple machine that is used mainly to split things apart.

An ax is a wedge that makes it easier to split wood.

You have experimented with five simple machines: lever, pulley, inclined plane, screw, and wedge. There's only one more simple machine. You can find it almost everywhere, even at home.

Wheeling It Up

You will need:
- two pencils
- wooden spool
- scissors
- string
- table
- tape
- two plastic cups
- marker
- twenty pennies

Push the pointed end of a pencil into each end of the spool. Make sure that the pencils fit tightly so that they do not twist or slide. Use a loop of string to hang each pencil from the edge of the table. Tape the free ends of the strings to the table.

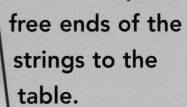

Make sure the pencils are level.

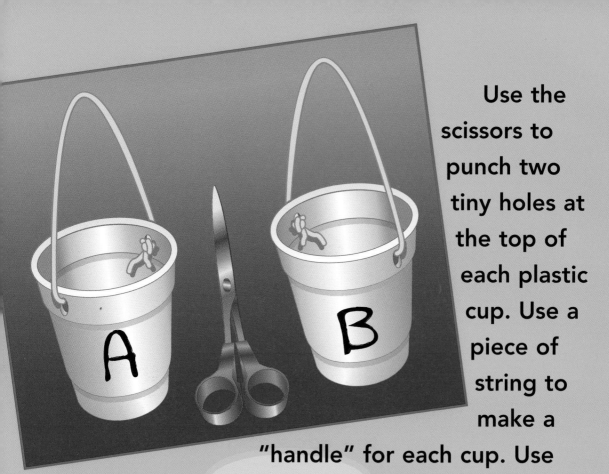

Use the scissors to punch two tiny holes at the top of each plastic cup. Use a piece of string to make a "handle" for each cup. Use the marker to label the cups A and B.

Tie a 2-foot (61-cm) long piece of string to the handle on cup A. Tape the free end of the string to the pencil. Turn the pencils away from you so that all the string wraps around the pencil. Tie another 2-foot (61-cm) long piece of string to the handle on cup B. Tape the free end of this string to the spool. Turn the pencils toward you so that all the string wraps around the spool.

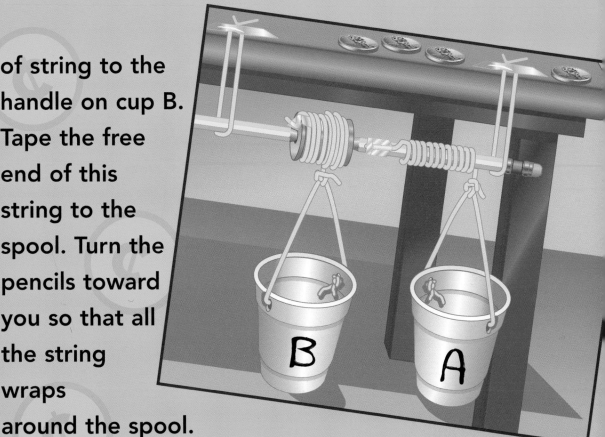

Place ten pennies in cup A. As you add each penny, the cup should drop to the ground. Cup B should remain near the spool. Add pennies one at a time to cup B. As you add each penny, cup B should drop to the ground. Notice that as cup B drops, cup A rises. How many pennies must you put in cup B to get cup A all the way up?

You should use fewer than ten pennies. The spool and pencils act as another simple machine called a wheel and axle. With the help of a wheel and axle, you need only a few pennies to lift a load of ten pennies. Like all other simple machines, a wheel and axle make work easier.

A pencil sharpener is a wheel and axle machine found in schools and homes.

Are All Machines Simple?

Although simple machines make work easier, there are many jobs they cannot do. When this happens, you may need to use a **compound machine** to get the job done. A compound machine is made by combining two or more simple machines. See how you can make a compound machine by combining two wheels and axles.

Gearing Up

You will need:
- modeling clay
- ruler
- twenty toothpicks
- two pencils
- table
- marker or tape

Flatten some modeling clay to make two wheels. One wheel should be 2 inches (5 cm) across. The other wheel should be 3 inches (8 cm) across. Stick eight toothpicks around the edge of the 2-inch (5-cm) wheel. Stick twelve toothpicks around the edge of the 3-inch (8-cm) wheel. Be sure that the toothpicks in both wheels are spaced apart the same distance and stick out the same length.

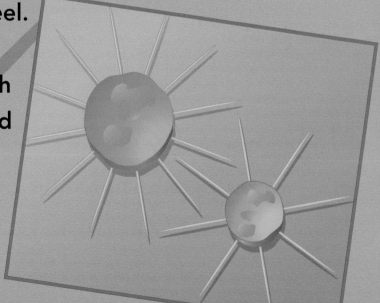

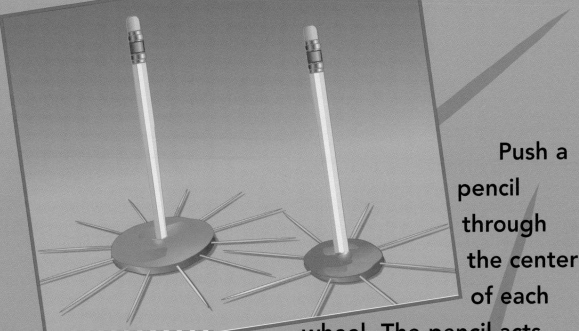

Push a pencil through the center of each wheel. The pencil acts like an axle. Squeeze the clay tightly around the pencils so that both the wheel and axle turn together. Place both wheels flat on the table so that their toothpicks overlap. Use a colored pen or tape to mark one toothpick on each wheel. Use the pencil to spin the larger wheel once around slowly. Count the number of turns the smaller wheel makes every time the larger wheel turns just once.

Notice that when the toothpicks on the larger wheel move, they cause the smaller wheel to move as well.

The toothpicks are like teeth on a wheel. A wheel with teeth is called a **gear**. Overlapping the gears of different-sized wheels causes them to move at different speeds. You should find that the smaller wheel makes more turns each time the larger wheel turns once. Gears are used to make one wheel move faster than the other. You may have a machine at home that uses gears to do just this.

An egg beater uses gears to make the blades spin faster than the handle you turn.

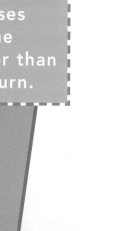

34

This power tool uses a gear (wheel) and a drill (screw) to make work easier.

You made a compound machine by combining two identical simple machines. Now see how a compound machine can also be made by combining two different kinds of simple machines.

Moving It Along

You will need:
- scissors
- ruler
- shoe box
- one sharpened pencil
- eight unsharpened pencils
- large book
- wooden block

Cut a 2-inch (5-cm) deep groove that extends almost from one end to the other end of the shoe box. Use the sharpened pencil to mark eight spots along each side of the shoe box. The spots should be evenly spaced and 1 inch (2.5 cm) from the top. The spots on both sides should line up with each other.

Use the scissors to poke a hole through each spot. Insert an unsharpened pencil into each pair of holes. The eight pencils should extend across the shoe box. Make sure that each hole is large enough so that the pencils can turn easily.

WALKERS
Color
Brown
Stock # Style #2

Place one end of the shoe box on the book. Set the wooden block on the two pencils closest to the book. Release the block and watch what happens. Placing the shoe box on the book makes it an inclined plane. The pencils in the shoe box act like wheels. Together, the inclined plane and wheels make a compound machine called a conveyor.

Can you locate the two simple machines that make up this conveyor?

A Rube Goldberg device uses simple machines to make a simple job more involved and more difficult. But simple machines are designed to make work easier. The six kinds of simple machines are the lever, pulley, inclined plane, screw, wedge, and wheel and axle. Combining two or more simple machines produces a compound machine. A compound machine can do work that a simple machine may not be able to do.

Fun With Simple Machines

Now that you have learned what simple machines are and how they work, here is a fun experiment to perform. You learned how a lever can make it easier to lift objects. Here is your chance to show your family and friends what you can do with the help of a lever.

Doing the Impossible

You will need:
- adult helper
- pencil
- table
- ruler
- ten pennies
- brick
- plank of 1-inch (2.5 cm) thick wood at least 4 feet (1.2 m) long

Place the pencil on the table. Lay the ruler across the pencil so that it teeters back and forth without touching the table. The pencil should be at about the middle, or the 6-inch (15-cm) mark on the ruler. Place eight pennies on the 12-inch (30-cm) end of the ruler. Place two pennies on the other end of the ruler.

The ruler should tip down toward the 12-inch (30-cm) end because the eight pennies weigh more than the two pennies.

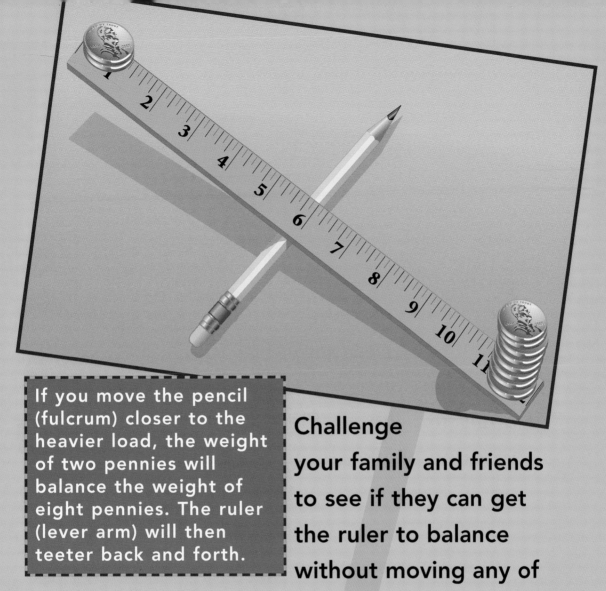

If you move the pencil (fulcrum) closer to the heavier load, the weight of two pennies will balance the weight of eight pennies. The ruler (lever arm) will then teeter back and forth.

Challenge your family and friends to see if they can get the ruler to balance without moving any of the pennies. Show them how easy it is to do this by moving the pencil closer to the 12-inch (30-cm) end of the ruler.

The ruler and pencil act like a lever. The ruler is the lever arm. The pencil is the fulcrum. By moving the fulcrum closer to the heavier end, you can balance the load so that the ruler does not touch the table. Now tell everyone that you can lift an adult into the air. Place the brick under the wooden plank, close to one end. Have an adult stand on the plank at that end. Then stand on the other end. Watch the lever lift the adult into the air easily.

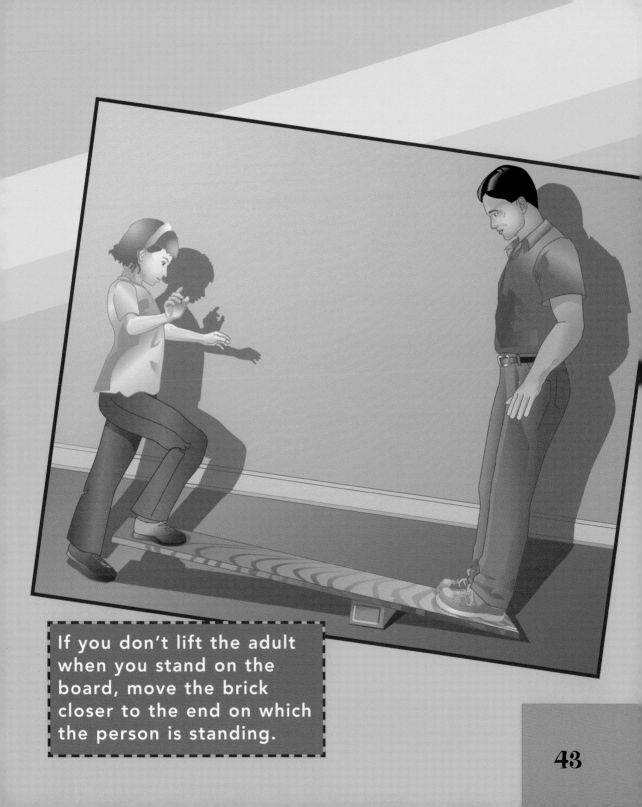

If you don't lift the adult when you stand on the board, move the brick closer to the end on which the person is standing.

To Find Out More

If you would like to learn more about simple machines, check out these additional resources.

Books

Hewitt, Sally. **Machines We Use.** Children's Press, 1998.

Jennings, Terry J. and Catherine Ward. **Forces and Machines.** Raintree Steck Vaughn, 1996.

Mason, Adrienne and Deborah Hodge. **Simple Machines.** Kids Can Press, 2000.

Nankivell-Aston, Sally and Dorothy Jackson. **Science Experiments with Simple Machines.** Franklin Watts, 2000.

Richards, Jon. **Work and Simple Machines.** Millbrook Press, 2000.

Wells, Robert E. **How Do You Lift a Lion?** Albert Whitman & Co., 1996.

Organizations and Online Sites

**Boston Museum
of Science**
Science Park
Boston, MA 021114
*http://www.mos.org/sln/
Leonardo/Inventors
Workshop/html*

This site lets you explore
Leonardo da Vinci's work
with machines performed
five hundred years ago.
See how a screw was used
to lift water from streams
to provide a supply of
drinking water.

**The Franklin Institute
Online**
Simple Machines
*http://www.fi.edu/qa97/
spotlight3/spotlight3.html*

Explore all six simple
machines and learn more
about them by checking
out the links on this site.

**Work Is Simple With
Simple Machines**
*http://www.ed.uri.edu/
smart96/elemsc/smart
machines/machine.html*

Here you will find several
activities using simple
machines, along with links
to related Web sites.

**The Official Rube
Goldberg Web Site**
*http://www.
rube-goldberg.com*

This where to begin if you
are interested in using simple machines to build a
Rube Goldberg device.

Important Words

compound machine machine made by combining two or more simple machines

fulcrum point at which the arm turns on a lever

gear wheel with teeth or points that stick out from its edges

inclined plane simple machine that looks like a ramp

lever simple machine that is usually straight, long, and narrow, such as a crowbar

lever arm part of a lever that can move

pulley simple machine that is made of a wheel with grooves through which a rope or chain passes

simple machine device that makes work easier to do

wedge simple machine that looks like a piece of pie

Index

Meet the Author

Salvatore Tocci is a science writer who lives in East Hampton, New York, with his wife, Patti. He was a high school biology and chemistry teacher for almost thirty years. As a teacher, he always encouraged his students to perform experiments to learn about science. His favorite simple machine is the wheel and axle. He loves watching wheels and axles run both the locomotives on his HO train layout and the movements on the antique pocket watches that he collects.

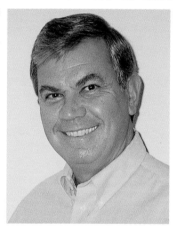